Losing Them, Finding You: Closure, Recovery, and Starting Over after Ghosting Relationships

By Dr. Michael A. Wright

Losing Them, Finding You: Closure, Recovery, and Starting Over after Ghosting Relationships/ Dr. Michael A. Wright

ISBN: **978-1-943616-77-0**

For permissions requests, write to the publisher at the address below:
MAWMedia Group, LLC
Los Angeles | Reno | Nashville
www.mawmedia.com

Contents

Losing Them & Finding Yourself Series: Introduction

I found myself intrigued by a curious meme that talked about moving on in the context of relationships. It presented 5 areas you would need to consider in your process of healing and moving forward after severing a relational tie. It applies even more to situations where you are left without a clear reason or a proper discussion and mutual decision-making process. Situations like ghosting in a relationship or a sudden firing from employment come to mind as examples.

Through sheer force of my will to overcome my own loss and answer questions for myself, I built the original 5 into 13 covering reasoning questions you want answered, character traits you become aware of as you learn to trust yourself again, growth habits you will want to practice, and mental flexibilities that allow you serenity and acceptance that you do not need all the answers. You only need to continue with purpose.

The Losing Them & Finding Yourself training is designed to help you recover, find resilience, and heal from a painful break-up, job loss, or other situation where the reasons are unclear, fabricated, or destructive. Loss can be difficult to process without information. It can leave you feeling lost, hurt, and uncertain about your future. The goal of this training is to help you find the fortitude required to recover and heal, even amid grief and uncertainty. Beyond that, you can cultivate the discernment, habits, and serenity to live an abundant life alone or in partnership with others.

Emotional Targets and Physical Actions

In these first two section Emotional Targets and Physical Actions are presented. This format aims to help learners navigate loss, build an individual vision, and manage change in productive ways while protecting their emotional space and respecting the autonomy of others. By the end of this training, learners will be equipped with the tools, strategies, and mindset necessary for healing, growth, and thriving even after losing someone or something important to them.

Each lesson in the training discusses how learners can apply intellect, judgment, and competence to their emotional management and well-being. These aspects work in tandem to help learners return to objectivity and balance the emotional chaos and physical mandates that must be overcome following a loss.

1. **Intellect**: Learning to engage in mental processes, such as problem-solving and rational thinking, to better understand and navigate the complex emotions associated with loss.
2. **Judgment**: Practicing reason and thoughtful decision-making without overthinking, ensuring decisions are made based on balanced considerations.
3. **Competence**: Trusting the evidence and research at hand, and the personal capabilities developed, rather than relying solely on gut reactions and emotions.

Emotional Targets works through the immediate and automatic thoughts of the moment in the context of hurt and loss.

The goal is to reframe toward transition and engage the emotional state that remind you of who you are alone. This sets the stage for healthy invitation to engage new opportunities.

Physical Actions serve to translate the principles of intellect, judgment, and competence into tangible, actionable tasks that learners can implement in their daily lives to facilitate healing, growth, and recovery. Because the body holds emotional energy in the muscles, physical action is both momentum and an opportunity for self-reflection.

For example, a lesson may outline specific strategies for:

1. Practicing mindfulness and meditation to enhance emotional awareness and stability.
2. Engaging in regular physical exercise to release stress and improve overall well-being.
3. Creating and maintaining a support network to foster social connection and emotional support.
4. Setting personal and professional goals to regain a sense of purpose and direction.

By merging Emotional Targets and Physical Actions into a cohesive lesson format, the Losing Them: Finding You Training provides learners with a comprehensive and holistic approach to overcoming loss, promoting personal growth, and re-establishing emotional stability.

Four Sections for Closure, Recovery, and Starting Over

Reasoning Needs: This section focuses on the reasoning needs that individuals have when experiencing a loss, such as ghosting, breakups, or job losses. It helps participants identify and understand their reasoning needs, which are essential for making sense of what has happened and for identifying tasks that can help individuals develop themselves beyond the pain of loss.

Reasoning Needs

1. Closure: You will not receive closure in every situation, but you can create it for yourself.
2. Explanation: Some actions don't have explanations. Some things cannot be explained.
3. Apology: Some people will not apologize because they can't.

Character Traits: This section explores the various character traits that can help individuals cope with loss and facilitate personal growth and healing. It includes discussions on traits such as ownership, protecting emotional space without hurting others, building an individual vision without isolating from collaboration, managing change productively without overbearing control, and respecting the autonomy of others needing change.

Character Traits

1. Ownership: What people do is about them not you.
2. Autonomy: You cannot change people no matter how much you think they need to change.
3. Personhood: Some people hurt others as a pre-emptive means of protecting themselves.

Mental Flexibilities are the cognitive and emotional skills that individuals can develop to maintain a growth mindset, adapt to new situations, and manage emotions effectively. These flexibilities include:

Mental Flexibilities

1. **Adaptability:** Embrace change with an open mind and a willingness to grow
2. **Self-Reflection:** Look within to understand your thoughts, emotions, and actions, fostering self-awareness and personal growth.
3. **Gratitude:** Appreciate the blessings in your life, cultivating a positive mindset and nurturing well-being.
4. **Flow:** Find true contentment coexisting with a desire for growth, improvement, and peace.

Developmental Targets. The last section present the developmental targets for flourishing intellect, judgment, and competence. They are presented as skills but may also be considered as the consistent emotional and physical targets that extend from a solid foundation of reasoning and character. Reflect upon what they suggest in practice and also what they inspire.

Growth Habits are the consistent practices and behaviors that individuals can incorporate into their daily lives to foster personal growth, build resilience, and adapt to change. The final section of the training focuses on the process of recovery, which involves personal growth, healing, and evolution. It provides guidance and support for participants as they navigate the challenges of loss and work towards building resilience, finding closure, and coping with grief.

Growth Habits

1. **Resourcefulness:** Use what you have to achieve what you want.
2. **Healing Space**: Continue to look for your tribe rather than attempting to fit.
3. **Productive Change:** Produce without aggression, without striving.
4. **Collaboration**: Create individual vision without isolating oneself from opportunities for collaboration.

Let's get started on this journey of recovery and growth together. Define your value by yourself alone and know that you are enough.

Losing Them Training and Its Purpose

Origins

The problem in these situations is that the fortitude required to recover, find resilience, and heal has most likely been damaged by the experience over time. In seeking to build on the relationship, you necessarily let go of elements of your independence and autonomy. You relied on the relationship in a mutual state of encouragement and community. Now, you are required to be mentally healthy even while grieving the loss and seeking to find yourself again in a world without a relationship.

The definition of self is difficult enough compounded by the grief that often interrupts your process. The other party has completely checked out. This leaves no opportunity for you to work through your despair, questions, or any anchors that allow you to cognitively process the loss.

Losing a relationship can significantly impact one's ability to recover, find resilience, and heal. When a relationship ends, your sense of self, independence, and autonomy may be deeply intertwined with the lost relationship. This loss can lead to a lack of clarity in your self-definition and make the healing process more difficult.

Reasoning Needs and Relationship Loss

The reasoning needs identified in the Losing Them training are essential for making sense of what has happened and for identifying tasks that can help individuals develop themselves beyond the pain of loss. These needs provide a framework for understanding and processing the emotions and experiences associated with relationship loss.

To cope with grief after a relationship loss, individuals can commit to going through the stages of grief as a necessary process, from denial to acceptance. This journey allows them to process their emotions and experiences and ultimately find healing and growth.

Reasoning Needs
1. Closure: In situations where closure cannot be achieved, such as ghosting or job loss without clear reasons, individuals can create closure by examining themselves and committing to self-development in areas they wish to expand and learn. This process allows them to find resolution and peace within themselves, even when external closure is unavailable.

2. Explanation: refers to the need for understanding the reasons behind the loss, such as the factors that led to a relationship ending or a job loss. Gaining an explanation can provide clarity, allowing individuals to learn from the experience and move forward with acceptance.

3. Apology: is the need for acknowledgment and validation of one's feelings and experiences related to the loss. Receiving an

apology, whether from the person responsible for the loss or through self-forgiveness, can facilitate emotional healing and promote personal growth.

Introducing Character Traits

Character traits are essential qualities that individuals can cultivate to help them cope with loss, facilitate personal growth, and foster healing. Incorporating these traits into one's daily life can make it easier to navigate difficult situations such as loss and change, while also building stronger relationships with others. Let's discuss some of the key character traits that can make a significant difference in our personal growth and healing journey.

By developing these character traits, one can also distinguish between the person who left and an ideal, compatible partner. When you cultivate these traits within yourself, you are better able to identify and attract individuals who share these values and qualities. This helps foster healthier, more fulfilling partnerships that are built on mutual growth and understanding.

In conclusion, focusing on these character traits enables individuals to not only navigate loss and personal growth more effectively but also to build stronger, healthier relationships with others. Embrace these traits, and you will find yourself on a path toward healing, resilience, and personal fulfillment.

Character Traits
1. Ownership: In the context of the Losing Them training, ownership means taking responsibility for one's growth and development separate from a relationship, working towards a clear and authentic expression of self. This sense of ownership

is crucial for personal growth and healing after a relationship loss.

2. Autonomy: To respect the autonomy of others, even when one thinks they need to change, individuals can offer complete information with a clear understanding of their own bias. By being open to scrutiny and allowing others to contemplate their options without undue influence, individuals can support the autonomous choices of others.

3. Personhood: refers to the development and recognition of one's unique identity and individuality, fostering self-awareness, self-esteem, and the establishment of healthy boundaries in relationships and interactions with others.

Growth & Healing

Ultimately there's a question in this for you. How will you grow and develop from this moment forward incorporating this experience in a productive way while recognizing and holding the pain that is inherent? The answer is more about your vision for the future, accepting the present rather than building on the past—the proposition you trusted before the situation changed. The answer is contrary to what you trusted the relationship to support. Change pulls away your expected foundation. That security is no more.

Now, in grief over losing the relationship with a sour experience of trust, change, and security, you must now trust in your individual vision, accept change as a positive forward, and reestablish security. The temptation, the inclination of self-protection, is to isolate that vision, control change, and pre-empt any potential threats to security. Resist. This is the damaged way the relationship governed their lives.

Growth Habits

1. Resourcefulness: Use what you have to achieve what you want. This growth habit involves making the most of your available resources, including skills, knowledge, connections, and assets. By being resourceful, you can find creative solutions to challenges and maximize your potential for success. To protect one's emotional space without hurting or discouraging others, individuals can make conscious decisions about the value of their relationships and the contributions they are willing to make. By establishing clear boundaries, communicating openly, and enforcing these boundaries in loving and consistent ways, individuals can maintain their emotional security without causing harm to others.

2. Healing Space: Continue to look for your tribe rather than attempting to fit. This habit encourages you to seek out like-minded individuals who share your values, goals, and interests. By surrounding yourself with a supportive community, you can foster personal growth, healing, and a sense of belonging.

3. Productive Change: Produce without aggression, without striving. This growth habit emphasizes the importance of adopting a non-striving approach to personal and professional development. By focusing on the process rather than the outcome, you can experience greater satisfaction, reduce stress, and cultivate a more balanced and sustainable approach to growth. To manage change productively without exerting overbearing control or possessiveness, individuals can practice non-striving and let go of fear-driven behaviors. By embracing the idea that they are enough on their own, they can engage in

relationships and achievements as outcomes of their consistent being, rather than desperate doing.

4. Collaboration: You can create an individual vision without isolating yourself from collaborative opportunities. You can inform and manage change in productive ways without overbearing control and possessiveness. You can protect your security including emotional space without striking to hurt or discourage others. You can build from the resources you have. Take time to grieve in your sustainable way. Then, assess your current situation for the resources available. Chart your process for vision, change, and security. To build an individual vision without isolating oneself from collaborative opportunities, individuals can recognize that collaboration comes in many forms beyond romantic relationships and employment. By identifying tasks needed to achieve their vision and adding collaborators as needed, individuals can maintain a balance between personal growth and collaborative connections.

Mental Flexibilities

Mental Flexibilities represents a key element of personal and professional growth. They are the practices and mindsets that keep us agile, curious, and continuously learning in an ever-changing world. By implementing Mental Flexibilities in your daily life, you are committing to continual learning and self-improvement in both your personal and professional life.

Implementing Mental Flexibilities involves seeking out new knowledge, skills, and experiences that assist you in growing and evolving as an individual. This is not limited to conventional academic learning or career skills, it also includes learning from day-to-day experiences, engaging with diverse perspectives, and actively seeking opportunities for personal development.

Key Elements of Mental Flexibilities

Being: This refers to the state of focusing on the present moment, remaining mindful of our attitudes, emotions, and reactions.

Mindfulness: This involves being fully present and attentive to the current situation, allowing one to respond to circumstances more wisely and with greater awareness.

Intentionality: This involves engaging in actions and decisions with clear purpose and direction, rather than simply reacting to circumstances.

By incorporating these key elements, Mental Flexibilities promote lifelong learning and adaptability, enabling you to handle change and uncertainty with resilience and positivity.

Engaging in Mental Flexibilities as daily habits starts from inward-being. Through mindfulness and intentionality, Mental Flexibilities can then be practiced in the mind and expressed through behavior. This continuous cycle of inner growth and outward application ensures a state of adaptability, reflectiveness, and gratitude— crucial traits in our rapidly evolving world.

1. Adaptability: Embrace change and remain flexible in the face of new challenges and opportunities. This mental flexibility involves being open to learning from new experiences and adjusting your strategies and goals as needed. By cultivating adaptability, you can more effectively navigate the uncertainties of life and maintain a positive outlook even when faced with setbacks.

2. Self-Reflection: Regularly assess your thoughts, emotions, and actions to gain insights into your strengths, weaknesses, and areas for improvement. This mental flexibility encourages you to engage in self-awareness practices, such as journaling, meditation, or seeking feedback from others. By consistently reflecting on your experiences, you can identify patterns and make more informed decisions about your personal and professional growth.

3. Gratitude: Cultivate an attitude of gratitude by regularly acknowledging and appreciating the positive aspects of your life. This mental flexibility can help you maintain a more optimistic mindset, improve your overall well-being, and foster stronger relationships with others. By practicing gratitude, you can shift your focus from what you lack to what you have, increasing your resilience and ability to cope with challenges.

4. Flow is an integration of adaptability, reflectiveness, and gratitude that can be cultivated through daily habits of engaging in Mental Flexibilities. By practicing mindfulness and intentionality, we develop an inner growth that can be expressed through our behavior. This cyclical process ensures both contentment and a desire for growth, even in the face of setbacks. It allows us to find enjoyment and fulfillment by realigning with our personal values and embracing a new normal based on gratitude and alignment.

Section I: Reasoning Needs

Reasoning Needs: This section focuses on the reasoning needs that individuals have when experiencing a loss, such as ghosting, breakups, or job losses. It helps participants identify and understand their reasoning needs, which are essential for making sense of what has happened and for identifying tasks that can help individuals develop themselves beyond the pain of loss.

Reasoning Needs
1. Closure: You will not receive closure in every situation, but you can create it for yourself.
2. Explanation: Some actions don't have explanations. Some things cannot be explained.
3. Apology: Some people will not apologize because they can't.

Closure: Writing the Ending

You will not receive closure in every situation, but you can create it for yourself.

Closure is the need to end the relationship rather than simply stop the relationship. Closure allows you to conclude the relationship with some semblance of completion involving patterns, rituals, or interactions that you can count as evidence of restoration or resolution. In short, closure is recovering what you invested in the relationship. The return may not be one-to-one or even equal, but your concern is that you can express yourself and your requirements. You desire the ability to count the costs with the person and negotiate a settlement.

When this experience is denied you, the feeling is one of being cheated. The resources, including emotional resources, that you invested are immediately counted as wasted. In any transaction, the worst feeling to walk away with is that of being cheated. It challenges your thoughts about your intellect, judgment, and competence. These form the scaffolding of your emotional targets and physical actions to be addressed for your healing.

Emotional Targets: Concluding with Emotional Intelligence, Discernment, and Capacity

Emotionally speaking, intellect, judgement, and competence translate to emotional intelligence, discernment, and capacity. Emotional intelligence is your ability to comprehend your emotions and those of others. In this situation, you want to learn to hold your emotions and define empathy as the ability to see the choices of others as reasonable—this even without an indication from them explicitly.

Discernment is the ability to determine the fit between any option and your goal and process. Everything that is possible is not advisable. That means that you can refuse feelings and explanations that don't fit the evidence and those that don't fit to inspire your progress.

Capacity is the ability of a person to account for their limitations and those of others. This reinforces that some people are not capable, don't have the depth, don't possess the ability to provide considerate, empathetic interaction. Release them from the requirement which also releases you from the expectation and disappointment associated with their inability to meet the expectation.

Physical Actions: Research, Experiments, and Staying Informed

Create closure for yourself with a combination of intellect, judgment, and competence. Physical actions that support intellect focus on the development of reasoning skills. Begin with evidence and variables that you can control. Sift through the available information you have. Match it with your emotion information. Apply any lessons learned to your personal development—the only process that you can control. If this includes ensuring your safety from the relationship, make certain to take the appropriate steps to address this need for security.

Judgment allows you to approach situations as experiments that seek additional information. Take your time to explore situations from a position of safety and a position of comparison. Establish an ideal including what you want from any given relationship. Give yourself the chance to evaluate new relationships and resources from a position of comparison with your ideal. Accept your evaluations as science and make decisions based on that science.

Competence is a concept to be informed continually. In addition to the basic fact-finding about the current situation, consider reading information, taking assessments, and reviewing your experiences in ways that support an increase of emotional competence. Emotional competence will result in emotional intelligence, social capacity, and interactive competence. Your competence will result in greater capability in every type of interaction.

Homework: Closure

Write a letter to yourself, outlining the closure you want to achieve from the situation. Include what closure means to you, why it is important, and what steps you can take to create closure for yourself.

Explanation: Answering Questions with Awareness

Some actions don't have explanations. Some things cannot be explained.

Especially when wrestling with high emotions, our minds desperately desire to reason. This translates into a need for a reason for the behavior of the other. Two things exist. At least two things.

First, the reason has very little to do with you. Even though they will attempt to insert you causally, your only fault is proximity to the failure. They will try to assign some of the blame to you attempting to prey upon your humility knowing that you are not perfect. The reason is tied solely to their choice. Stated simply, they chose this action. Your choice, now, is how to respond. Even in your most regrettable interactions with the other, understand that you don't hold the ability to force their hand. Adults own their choices no matter what influenced their decision-making.

Second, explanations offered in this context are rarely long and complex. The process of choice is a matter of desire, opportunity, and execution. The Desire is simply wanting a certain thing. If one does not want it, one does not seek it. Opportunity is something that comes along and gives you the chance to put your desire into action. No matter what the pressure is, Opportunity is only capitalized upon by Desire. Execution, of course, is doing the thing. Execution is also recognizing what is done and confirming it. What's most important is the underlying desire.

This brings you to the final resting place for all reasons. It was done because the other wanted to do it. Resist the need to ascertain where the desire originated. That is work that you should not be doing on another person unless you are trained and paid to do so. That profiling energy is better spent on You.

Emotional Targets: Behavior Knowledge, Listening, and Process

Intellect, judgment, and competence with explanation needs translates into behavior knowledge, listening, and process. Know that human behavior suggests some basic principles about how humans interact. If you want something, you do what you need to do. You are motivated intrinsically. You push yourself without the need for external motivators. If you are not going after it, you don't want it bad enough. Your emotional target is to feel your desire and recognize theirs.

Listening here is critical. When a person communicates their desires through their behaviors, pay attention. Listening is not just hearing. It is adjusting your expectations and interactions according to what you are discerning. Commit to listening for your own needs. Admit to them without determination of their pros and cons. Accept them as yours.

Process competence is another critical skill. You must know how IT works whatever the IT is. The basics are humans and systems. People behave in predictable ways. Systems follow discernible patterns. Your emotional target is toward a feeling of control. You can't control the situation or the actors, but your sense of control comes from knowing people and systems over time. As you see the patterns, note them. Expect them to repeat. Plan and act accordingly.

Now, you can mold your motivations to fit your desired outcomes. You are primed to seek what you want authentically or to put in the work to change your perspective, mindset, or habits to better fit your desired outcomes. Heal from what the other is plagued with: a disconnect between spoken words and behavior.

Physical Actions: Attend, Judge, Choose

Intellectually, process the knowledge you have gained from experience. You want an explanation from their lips, but you have one from their actions and your experiences. The explanation you hold may be better than any explanation they may give with their potential to lie, misdirect, rationalize, or otherwise state what they think you want to hear.

In my experience and observations of clients, you have been told from their lips. You most likely did not listen. You lacked the context to hear them fully when they told you who they were and their pattern failings. They may have related a story about an ex or a troubling childhood memory. Remember the conclusions they drew and the personality traits they chose to incorporate. The negatives were not targeting you, so you may not have registered the deficit and immaturity. Now, in your search for closure, you can hear their words and judge without the filters.

Judgment often feels like you are applying bitterness and aggression. You may feel those, but executing wise judgment is a positive character trait. Preserving your peace is a mental health activity. Limit interactions. Refuse to "forgive" in ways that violate safety and subject you to dishonesty. I heard a client tell the story of leaving a verbally abusive relationship fearing that it would become physical. She stole away after an argument without the partner's knowledge. A couple of weeks later, after threats and incessant calling, she agreed to meet with him alone in the home they once shared. No! Don't allow time to lull you into an unsafe situation. Her fears are backed up by science. Her actions were dangerous.

Turn your energy inward to develop new coping rather than second-guessing your character. Refuse to allow their words to penetrate. They will tell you that a "good person" will accept them, listen, or provide another chance. This is a time to listen to the past actions as a predictor of future behavior. Monitor carefully. Inward focus can be overwhelming and self-critical. Your task is to recite affirmations, rehearse positivity, and nurture You all while remaining safe. Learn during this moment to be alone. If that feels impossible, connect with a trusted friend or professional support.

Competence with explanations is about regaining a sense of control. It is knowledge of patterns that release you from anxiety about being blindsided by the other person. Believe the patterns. Prepare for them. Maintain safety and peace above all. Never allow a sense of love and loyalty to make you a repeat target. Choose health, peace, and serenity.

You do not owe anything to anyone. It is a fallacy to think that you must give others your attention, time, and energy. It is a lie that you are a bad person for setting a firm boundary against giving them an audience. Even if you are interested in them, they must not be your priority. YOU are your priority. You, healthy, choose who to share You with and how much to give in any interaction.

The critical explanation you need is a competent return to You, your habits, interests, and love of You. If you do not have this knowledge available, spend the time to identify and develop these explanations that become expressions of You. This explanation will improve all your interactions romantic and otherwise.

Homework: Explanation
Create a list of questions you have about the situation that you feel need to be explained. Then, research and write down possible answers to those questions. Focus on accepting that some things cannot be explained and finding peace in that.

Apology: Shifting from Their Feelings to Yours

Some people will not apologize because they can't.

You most likely do not want an apology at this point. Like the explanation needs, you are not interested in more lies and attempts to sign you up for more trauma. The need is for them to experience the pain of what they did—to genuinely feel remorse and regret for what they did. The challenge in ghosting situations is that they make no effort to provide this communication. Even with non-ghosting breakups, it may be healthier to forego these interactions not wanting to offer opportunity for your own feelings to betray you into another chance for them. The truth is that they are not sorry. They made intentional choices for their benefit alone.

Apology is a process that must be intentional from start to completion: Articulate a position. Argue merits toward consensus, and Acceptance of the outcome whether agreement or agreement to disagree. The problem in toxic relationships is that acceptance is requested (even required) without the other steps of articulation or argument. Blind acceptance leads to additional conflict as considerations thought to be common understanding are violated due to ignorance. In other words, people do things wrong saying that they misunderstood though the rules were never stated.

The true utility of the apology need is not in the person offering or not offering. The utility is in the ability. An apology is "to regret or feel remorse for an inability to do something." That ability deficit covers both your need for an explanation and your need for an apology. By not giving you the love, safety, and security, you deserve, the other has confirmed that they are not able to provide for your health and well-being. Whether you have the verbal expressions of their feeling, your knowledge of your worth affirms their regret. Your knowledge of your authenticity and loyal intention affirms their remorse. They are sorry in the character-defining sense of the word. They can't apologize. They lack the ability. They lack the character.

Emotional Targets: Reciprocity, Balance, and Character

Intellect, judgment, and competence with apology needs translate into reciprocity, balance, and character. The target of an apology should be the emotional well-being of the injured party, not just intellectual understanding or acceptance of the facts. The objective of an apology is to restore dignity and respect, not simply provide a rational explanation or excuse.

Insincere apologies tend to intellectualize and minimize the injury by focusing on external factors such as "mistakes were made," or knowledge deficits as in, "I was unaware." Character excuses can also be offered such as, "I am only human." This tendency is evident in apologies for unintentional acts and for intentional acts.

Reciprocity, balance, and character are all emotional targets that are intertwined with the need for a genuine apology. Reciprocity refers to the idea that when we invest time, energy, and emotions into a relationship, we expect a similar level of investment from the other person. In the context of an apology, reciprocity means that we expect the other person to acknowledge the harm they have caused and to make a genuine effort to make things right.

Balance is another emotional target related to apologies. When someone has hurt us, we may feel a sense of imbalance in the relationship - as if the other person holds more power or control. An apology can help to restore balance by allowing us to assert our needs and boundaries and to feel that our feelings and experiences are being validated.

Finally, character is an emotional target that is closely tied to the ability to offer a genuine apology. When someone lacks the ability or willingness to apologize, it can be a sign of a deeper character flaw, such as a lack of empathy or accountability. On the other hand, a genuine apology can demonstrate that the other person values our well-being and is willing to take responsibility for their actions. This awareness can enable you to discern the character of a person and restore your sense of trusting yourself. You reclaim your self-sufficiency and see clearly despite your pain.

In situations where the other person is unable or unwilling to offer a genuine apology, it may be necessary to find closure and healing through other means. This could involve focusing on self-care, seeking support from loved ones or a therapist, or finding ways to forgive and move on without the other person's involvement. Ultimately, the emotional targets of reciprocity, balance, and character remind us of the importance of healthy, respectful relationships and the need for genuine apologies when harm has been done.

Physical Actions: Require, Contribute, Note

In your quest to maintain healthy relationships, there are specific physical actions you can focus on: requiring reciprocity, contributing equitably, and noting interactions without keeping score. These actions are vital in building and repairing relationships, and they involve tangible behaviors that foster understanding and growth.

Firstly, requiring reciprocity sets the stage for a balanced exchange between you and the other person. It involves communicating your needs and expectations, making it clear that a sincere effort from both parties is required. Requiring reciprocity means seeking actions that demonstrate the other person's commitment to repairing the relationship. It may involve open and honest communication, spending quality time together, or small acts of kindness that show they are invested in making things right.

Contributing equitably is another physical action that cultivates a healthy relationship. It is easy to fall into the trap of feeling like you are carrying the burden of the relationship's growth alone. However, by actively contributing to the relationship's well-being, you establish a sense of balance and equality. By offering support, understanding, and flexibility, you actively contribute to the emotional and overall growth of the relationship. This balance fosters trust, respect, and a deeper connection.

Additionally, noting interactions without keeping score is crucial for personal character development. It involves recognizing and appreciating the lessons and insights gained from previous experiences. When you focus on personal growth, you shift your perspective from keeping score to embracing the opportunities for learning and self-improvement. Noting interactions without keeping score means focusing on the positive aspects of the relationship and acknowledging the progress made, rather than harboring resentment or seeking tit-for-tat actions.

Ultimately, these physical actions of requiring reciprocity, contributing equitably, and noting interactions without keeping score contribute to the overall health and strength of your relationships. These actions empower you to set boundaries, expect a balanced commitment from others, and nurture personal character growth. By actively engaging in these behaviors, you create a foundation for stronger, healthier relationships that foster understanding, trust, and lasting connection.

Homework: Apology

Write a letter to the person who hurt you, expressing how their actions affected you and what you would like them to apologize for. Then, write a follow-up letter to yourself, detailing what you learned from the experience and how you can move forward without receiving an apology.

Section II: Character Traits

Character Traits: This section explores the various character traits that can help individuals cope with loss and facilitate personal growth and healing. It includes discussions on traits such as ownership, protecting emotional space without hurting others, building an individual vision without isolating from collaboration, managing change productively without overbearing control, and respecting the autonomy of others needing change.

Character Traits
1. Ownership: What people do is about them not you.
2. Autonomy: You cannot change people no matter how much you think they need to change.
3. Personhood: Some people hurt others as a pre-emptive means of protecting themselves.

Ownership: Allow Them Their Faults

What people do is about them not you.

What people do is about them not you. Just as you make decisions with motivation, intention, and desire in mind, so do others. Allow them to own their choices and the character evidenced from their actions. When you step up and take ownership of your life, you are taking responsibility for every choice you make and every action that follows. Owning your life means making a conscious decision to never place blame on anyone or anything outside of yourself. You must expect this boundary of self-awareness and mutual respect from those you deal with.

You will find that when you take ownership of your life, there is no need for excuses or explanations for anything that happens because you are fully accountable for the decisions you make. Grow to recognize the process of your decision-making and how you can intentionally expand your choices through education, partnership, and collaboration.

As a character trait, ownership offers a critical mix of accountability and leadership. You may not always make people feel comfortable. Sometimes it is your actions that upset another person even when you do not intend to. Those who exhibit ownership will own their actions even while understanding that they are not responsible for how the other person interprets the actions. Not responsible, but concerned enough to make a change for the sake of the relationship or caring enough to explain their point of view and why this course of action will continue. Either provides a clear character profile for you to determine fit.

Emotion Targets: Motivation, Intention, and Influence

Intellect, judgment, and competence with ownership needs translate into Motivation, Intention, and Influence. When we own something, we feel connected to it--we care about its safety and security, as well as its value to us personally. Ownership can be applied to many aspects of our lives: possessions (e.g., "I own this book"), relationships ("I own my husband"), emotions ("I feel like I own my anger"), goals ("my goal is my own"). Ownership is also related to responsibility; if something belongs to us then we have an obligation toward it--to care for it appropriately, protect it from harm or damage when possible, make decisions based on what's best for all parties involved rather than just ourselves alone.

Motivation feels like a push toward accountability because it is the driving force that propels us towards achieving our goals. It's the inner voice that reminds us of the importance of taking responsibility for our actions and the consequences that follow. With motivation, we feel a sense of empowerment that comes from being accountable for our actions. It is this sense of accountability that gives us the strength to push through obstacles and overcome challenges, ultimately leading to greater success.

Intention feels like decisiveness in your daily life because it's the foundation upon which we build our lives. It's the deliberate choice to pursue our goals with focus and direction. When we set clear intentions, we gain clarity and purpose, leading to a more fulfilling and meaningful life. Intention is the force that drives our actions, helping us stay focused and determined in the face of challenges. It's the key to achieving our goals and living a life that is aligned with our values and beliefs.

Influence feels like powerful leadership where you stand as an example of progress because it is the ability to inspire and motivate others towards positive change. When we lead by example, we set the standard for others to follow. Influence is the power to make a difference, to create positive change in the world around us. It's the ability to inspire others to be their best selves, to strive for excellence, and to overcome obstacles. Influence is the foundation of effective leadership, and it's what enables us to create a better world for ourselves and those around us.

Physical Actions: Resolve, Seek Help, and Help Others

Motivation looks like words and behaviors that right the wrongs we have committed. When we recognize our mistakes, it is natural to feel guilt and shame. However, simply feeling remorse is not enough. True motivation comes from taking action to correct our mistakes and make amends for our wrongdoings. Whether we need to apologize, make restitution, or change our behavior, motivation drives us to do what is necessary to make things right.

In relationships lost, motivation also involves learning from our mistakes and moving forward. We must examine our actions and reactions to understand what went wrong and how we can improve in the future. Motivation helps us to let go of the past and focus on building a better future.

Intention looks like determined action to improve through therapy, coaching, and coursework based on your self-improvement focus. It involves setting clear goals and taking steps to achieve them. Whether we are working on personal growth, career advancement, or improving our relationships, intention provides the focus and direction we need to succeed.

Intentional self-improvement often involves seeking help from others. Therapy, coaching, and coursework provide the knowledge, skills, and support we need to make meaningful progress towards our goals. Intention helps us to stay on track, even when the going gets tough.

Influence looks like an agenda of both self-development and intentional support of others. We all have the power to influence those around us, whether we realize it or not. When we focus on self-improvement, we become a positive example for others to follow. We can inspire and motivate others to make positive changes in their own lives.

At the same time, influence also involves intentionally supporting others. When we reach out to those who are struggling, we can help them find the support and resources they need to succeed. Influence is about making a positive impact on the world around us, by both improving ourselves and supporting those around us.

Homework: Ownership

Write a list of actions that the other person took that hurt you. Next to each action, write down how you can reframe it as being about them, not you. Focus on accepting that their actions are not a reflection of your worth.

Autonomy: Rediscovering Your Choices

You cannot change people no matter how much you think they need to change.

Change in the person is not the reality you may think it to be. You are attracted to the person by something that is not the change you hope to effect. You are attracted to the project, but the exchange desired is not their difference in behavior. That's why these relationships are always flawed. If they change, you will no longer have the external motivation you once had. Your achievement would make your interactions less visceral and meaningful. If they do not change, you risk toxicity and resentment as nothing you do seems to make a difference in their choice behavior.

In the face of a breakup, you may hear others ask you a loaded question. "Why now? They must have been doing what you like at some point in the beginning." This is a tricky consideration. Were you fooled by something that they projected? The better question is why you were willing to be fooled. You were willing because you were trading your better judgement for something that they offered that you wanted. The challenge for most is that we are not in tune with ourselves. We desire beauty, status, control, or some fleeting form of security.

Most likely, the change that you are experiencing in the person is not a change that you desired or worked toward. The change is your realization that your desire is not being met AND you are not willing to forego your pleasure or satisfaction any longer.

As a character trait, autonomy is the decision to live according to an objective standard rather than your desires. Understand that this is not a demand from more from others. Like much of character, it is a demand from You. You must raise the bar for your performance, your self-love, your ability to be alone and love it, your commitment to reclaim yourself. Your impact is not hindered by them or anyone else. Your impact is up to you. Take the moral stand and live up to your full potential regardless of what others choose to do.

Emotional Targets: Confirmation, Serenity, Self-Focus

In your pursuit of emotional targets, you may find yourself seeking confirmation, serenity, and solitude. Sometimes, when we enter a relationship, we focus on changing the other person to fit our desires. We may hope to end bad habits or to see them become more communicative or assertive. However, it's essential to realize that we cannot force others to change. We must learn to accept others for who they are and what they bring to the relationship.

Confirmation is about understanding that the behavior of the other person reflects who they are, rather than trying to change them. When we accept someone's character without the desire to change them, we can make an informed decision about compatibility and the potential for growth together. It's important to rely on observations of their behavior to make decisions about the relationship.

Serenity is achieved by releasing the need to control situations and outcomes. It's about protecting your emotional and physical space while allowing the other person to be themselves. You can't be responsible for the other person's behavior, but you can choose to take care of yourself, your own goals, and needs. This hallmark builds a sustainable relationship between you and the other person by creating a comfortable and healthy dynamic in the relationship.

Self-Focus is the final emotional target; it is about focusing on yourself and your personal development instead of changing others. This means acknowledging that your attraction to them could be based on admiration for their character traits, personality, or intelligence. By getting alone and focusing on your own growth, you can achieve confirmation of your worth and value, as well as personal development. This admiration is healthy as long as you don't try to mimic or become the person you admire.

Ultimately, the key to emotional targets is autonomy; the decision to live according to your standards and values, independent of the desires of others. By doing so, you affirm your worth, your potential for personal growth, and achieve emotional targets of confirmation, serenity, and solitude. These three targets are grounded in self-awareness and contribute to relationships based on respect and emotional freedom.

Physical Actions: Observe, Meditate, Get Alone

To fully achieve the physical targets of confirmation, serenity, and personal development, it is important to recognize their close connection to our emotional well-being. These physical targets require intentional actions and practices that position you to observe, release control, and focus on self-development.

One step to achieve this is to physically position yourself to watch and learn, interpreting the behaviors of others. Taking a step back and objectively observing the situation can provide valuable insights and understanding. By physically removing yourself from the situation if necessary, you can create space for reflection and evaluation of the dynamics at play. This can lead to greater clarity and perspective, aiding in the process of releasing control.

Releasing control can be facilitated by practicing mindfulness and meditation. Meditate to arrest your automatic thoughts toward reprisal, revenge, and second-guessing yourself. Engaging in these practices allows you to quiet your mind and let go of the need to control every aspect of the situation. By focusing on the present moment and relinquishing attachment to specific outcomes, you can cultivate a sense of peace, serenity, and acceptance. This will free you from the burden of trying to manipulate or direct the actions of others.

Self-development also requires physical actions, such as sequestering yourself. This can involve engaging in physical activities that promote your well-being, such as exercise, engaging in healthy eating habits, and prioritizing self-care practices such as getting enough sleep and dedicating time for personal reflection. By taking care of your physical health, you are laying a foundation for overall well-being and personal growth.

Crucially, self-love is a vital component of self-development. Learning to love yourself involves accepting and embracing who you are, with both your strengths and weaknesses. It also means seeking support, such as counseling, to work through any emotional or mental blocks that may hinder your self-love and personal growth. By addressing these barriers, you can cultivate a healthier relationship with yourself and create space for personal development.

Homework: Autonomy

Write down a list of things you have tried to do to change the other person, but ultimately failed. Next to each item, write down an action you can take to focus on your own growth and well-being, rather than trying to change someone else.

Personhood: Stoking Your Emotional Intelligence

Some people hurt others as a pre-emptive means of protecting themselves.

You have heard the phrase, "Hurt people hurt people." It is true. The core of our discussion will center on the why. Most often, the hurt of others is an attempt to save self. But more practically, the veracity of the aggression displayed in the hurting is observed as meanness. The actual origin is much more dangerous: fear.

Fear is much more dangerous because evil or mean behavior is somewhat reasonable and intentional. Fear, however, is irrational and self-perpetuating. That means it is unpredictable and builds intensity on itself. You know this if you have ever been in a scary situation. One person screams and sets off a chain reaction where others are screaming and running even if they don't know what the threat is. Fear in this context   is   much   the   same.

The personhood described here as a character trait is a mix of identity and identity in application—what we typically call personality. Some may say, "That's just the way I am. Take it or leave it." They offer you an honest choice. Feel fully empowered to leave it if the fit is uncomfortable. If their attempts at protecting themselves are toxic, you owe it to yourself to build distance from the toxicity. Be sick of it before you become sick because of it.

Emotional Targets: Recovery, Emotion Management, Mood Management

Intellect, judgment, and competence with ownership needs translate into Recovery, Emotion Management, Mood Management. Learn your triggers. But also learn your rejuvenators, your recreation, and your recalibrations.

When you're feeling drained, you need rejuvenators. These are experiences that replace your drained energy and help you feel refreshed. They can be anything from eating a snack to taking a nap. I like to think of them as the opposite of drains—they don't take any energy away from you, but instead give you more.

Recreation is the experience of remembering your purpose. It's a time when you can reflect on what makes you happy, what brings meaning to your life, and why it's important to keep going. Recreation is more than just fun. It's an important part of your well-being, because it helps you remember why you're doing what you're doing in the first place. When I'm feeling drained and need to recharge my batteries, I like to take a break from work and do something that's purely recreational—something that I enjoy doing for its own sake.

Recalibration is a standard that organizes and modulates your moods. It helps you realize that there are times when things might not go as planned, but they will still be okay in the end because how you start is necessarily how you will end. Recalibration helps you to remember that the world will continue to spin whether or not you keep up with it, so there's no need to rush. It reminds you that your value is not dependent upon how much work gets done in a day or week—or even a year. Recalibration gives you a chance to step back from your situation and figure out what's important and what isn't, so when you return to the task at hand, it will be easier to focus on what really matters.

Physical Actions: Stop, Recreate, Recalibrate

Learn to stop. Stopping is a skill that can support discipline, consistency, and motivation in your life. Many people believe that starting is the hard part, but often it's the fear of not being able to stop that holds us back. We worry about missing out on something if we begin. This fear of missing out on our lives can hinder our progress. If you tend to hyperfocus, learning to channel that neurodivergence can help you accomplish more.

So, take a moment to stop. Pause what you're doing and give yourself a break. Treat yourself to 15 minutes to an hour of something that is purely fun and energizing. Release yourself from the pressures of work and engage in activities that bring you joy and playfulness.

Recreate. Find activities that are enjoyable and rejuvenating. Just as you fuel your body, recognize the need to fuel your soul. Identify what brings you spiritual nourishment, what feeds your soul. Our emotions have a physical impact on our bodies, and we may be more aware of this impact when it is negative. We might experience aches from poor posture or typing, but we may be less aware of the energy boost we get from completing a project or having a good night's sleep.

One physical manifestation of emotional management is to stand, sit, or lie within the experience of satisfaction and soak up the positivity, endorphins, and energy of the moment. This is the difference between simply engaging in an activity and truly experiencing it. It's the difference between being productive and being fulfilled. You can have both when you are intentional about both.

Recalibrate. Take time to reflect on the big picture of your life in the context of your values and desires. Recalibration allows you to see the forest instead of just the individual trees of daily tasks. You may find that you need to recalibrate your goals and priorities more often than once a year. I recommend doing it at least every quarter. By regularly reassessing and realigning your goals, you can ensure that you are on track and living in accordance with your values.

By incorporating these physical actions of stopping, recreating, and recalibrating into your life, you can better manage your emotions, find a sense of fulfillment, and live a more purposeful and balanced life. Remember to take breaks, engage in activities that bring you joy, and regularly reflect on your goals and priorities.

Homework: Personhood

Write down a list of ways the other person hurt you as a means of protecting themselves. Then, write down ways you can protect yourself without hurting others. Focus on finding healthy ways to set boundaries and protect your emotional space.

Section III: Mental Flexibilities

Mental Flexibilities are the cognitive and emotional skills that individuals can develop to maintain a growth mindset, adapt to new situations, and manage emotions effectively. These flexibilities include:

Mental Flexibilities
1. **Adaptability:** Embrace change with an open mind and a willingness to grow
2. **Self-Reflection:** Look within to understand your thoughts, emotions, and actions, fostering self-awareness and personal growth.
3. **Gratitude:** Appreciate the blessings in your life, cultivating a positive mindset and nurturing well-being.
4. **Flow:** Find true contentment coexisting with a desire for growth, improvement, and peace.

Adaptability: Finding Joy in Transition

You can embrace change with an open mind and a willingness to grow. Instead of resisting new situations or challenges, you can view them as opportunities for personal and professional development. By cultivating adaptability, you can cope better with uncertainty and unexpected changes in life, allowing you to become more resilient and capable in the face of adversity.

Adaptability, defined as the ability to cope and thrive amidst changes, is a foundational aspect of your personal and professional development. By fostering adaptability, you can better handle uncertainty, face challenges head-on, and ultimately build resilience.

When it comes to loss, adaptability becomes even more crucial. Encountering loss requires you to adjust to a new way of living and embrace a new norm. Through your intellect, judgment, and competence with adaptability, you can find joy amid this transition.

Emotional Targets: Allowing, Positivity, and Non-Striving

By embracing the targets of allowing, positivity, and non-striving, you open yourself up to a more flexible and adaptive approach to life. Through this mindset, you will find yourself better equipped to handle the ups and downs that come with change. Remember to be open-handed in your approach, embracing the invitation for growth and learning. Calibrate your judgment to focus on positive outcomes, celebrating the opportunities that change brings. Finally, trust in your ability to adapt and be resilient in the face of challenges. By embodying these emotional targets, you can cultivate greater peace, happiness, and fulfillment in your life.

Allowing. Take the time to truly understand the importance of adaptability in your life. Contemplate the role that change plays in your personal growth and overall well-being. Recognize that resisting change often leads to stress and discomfort, while embracing adaptability can pave the way to resilience and growth. Holding onto something tightly doesn't guarantee that it will stay in your hand if it's meant to be let go. Instead, open your hand with a sense of invitation, creating the space for what is meant to be yours.

Positivity. Shift your mindset and incorporate judgment calibrated for positive outcomes when faced with change. Instead of viewing changes as disruptions or inconveniences, start seeing them as opportunities for exploration and learning. Practice discernment in how you perceive people and circumstances, separating what you have control over from what you cannot change. Cultivate a sense of serenity and acceptance for the things that are beyond your control.

Non-Striving. Trust in the power of adaptability as a primary factor for emotional resilience. Draw upon your personal experiences, seek out research data, and utilize the tools available to enhance your readiness to adjust to new circumstances and overcome the challenges that come with loss or change. Shift your mindset from tirelessly striving to achieve specific outcomes and instead focus on inviting opportunities and transformations into your life.

Physical Actions: Work Smarter, Solve Problems, Embrace Uncertainty

Embracing change with an open mind and seeking growth are essential in putting adaptability into action. By cultivating a growth mindset and approaching new challenges as opportunities for learning and development, you can work smarter and enhance your adaptability. Instead of viewing change as insurmountable, choose to learn from the experience and develop novel approaches. Trust in your competence and persevere, despite any criticism or skepticism from others. Adaptability goes beyond just surviving change; it allows you to thrive in the face of it.

Work Smarter. Engage your intellect, make judicious decisions, and rely on your capabilities to foster adaptability. By doing so, you not only comfort yourself following a loss but also promote personal growth and resilience.

Solve Problems. Enhancing problem-solving skills is key to adapting effectively to change. Identify the issue at hand, generate possible solutions, evaluate them, and implement the most favorable one. Problem-solving skills enable you to navigate through challenges and find innovative ways to adapt and thrive.

One obstacle to adaptability is high stress levels. Stress can hinder your ability to adapt and make effective decisions. Practice managing stress effectively by incorporating mindfulness, meditation, or physical exercise into your routine. These stress-management techniques can help balance your emotions and keep you open to change.

Embrace Uncertainty. Uncertainty is an unavoidable aspect of life, and learning to embrace it is crucial for adaptability. Recognize uncertainty as a natural element of life and an opportunity to develop flexibility and resilience. Break away from routines and seek diverse experiences. Engage in new activities, meet different people, and expose yourself to various cultures and perspectives. This broadens your horizons and makes it easier for you to adapt to different situations.

Adaptability Homework Assignment

For the next week, engage in one activity that pushes you out of your comfort zone daily. This could be anything from trying a new cuisine to learning a new skill or starting a conversation with a stranger. Write a brief 100-word reflection on what you learned after the week, focusing on how the experience affected your outlook on change and your ability to adapt to new or challenging situations.

Self-Reflection: Look Internally to Create External Realities

Self-Reflection involves looking inward to better comprehend our thoughts, emotions, and actions. Regular self-reflection fosters self-awareness, leading to a deeper understanding of our motives, which can help us discover blind spots and areas for improvement. By recognizing our patterns, understanding their causes, and revisiting our reactions, we gain a clearer perception of ourselves and our interactions with the world, promoting personal growth and emotional health.

In this lesson, we delve into the purview of self-reflection, a practice that cultivates self-awareness and facilitates personal growth. Briefly put, self-reflection involves introspectively examining our thoughts, emotions, and actions. It's an indispensable tool that offers us a clearer understanding of our motives and can illuminate areas for improvement.

Emotional Targets: Pattern Identification, Humility, Emotional Resilience

Working through loss often encourages us to look inward and engage in self-reflection, a process that assists us in understanding our experiences and fostering emotional resilience. In practicing self-reflection, the key emotional targets—intellect, judgment, and competence—translate into pattern identification, humility, and emotional resilience.

Pattern Identification. Comprehending the potential patterns in our reactions to loss is crucial. Analyze why your mind processes certain events with greater impact and why we respond in specific ways. Devote time to understanding the emotional and behavioral cycles that take place when confronted with loss, aiming to develop a deeper self-awareness. This may require some trauma work with a competent therapist.

Humility. Approach your thoughts, feelings, and actions with a sense of humility and balanced judgment; self-reflection is about gentle exploration, not self-deprecation. Appreciate your strengths and recognize areas for growth without being overly critical or harsh. When your voice inside your head speaks to you, make it a cheerleader promoting your ability and motivating you toward action.

Emotional Resilience. Trust in the power of self-reflection as a tool that contributes to emotional well-being and develops coping mechanisms during times of loss. Deliberately focus on fostering improvement in the areas identified through self-reflection, and aim to build resilience and emotional stability. The first step is a decision to heal, which often takes you through the grief process to walk through and feel the hurt. Don't shy away from the pain. It will be there anyway. You will do well to address it intentionally.

Physical Actions: Journaling, Sharing, Grief Work

To effectively facilitate self-reflection, it's important to engage in physical actions that translate our emotional targets into tangible steps. By implementing these actions, we can navigate the aftermath of loss with resilience and understanding. Regularly engaging in self-reflection not only promotes healing and personal growth but also strengthens our emotional and psychological well-being.

Start by journaling

Writing about your thoughts, feelings, and experiences can serve as a therapeutic outlet, allowing you to express yourself freely and honestly. By recording your reflections, you can trace your emotional journey and identify patterns over time. Consider incorporating mindful meditation into your practice. This technique enables you to focus on your inner state without judgment, simply observing and understanding. Set aside 10-15 minutes each day for mindful reflection. To deepen your self-reflection, ask yourself questions like: "Why did I react that way?" "What can I learn from this situation?" and "How does this align with my values and personal goals?"

Share your gifts

Find ways to engage with others and share your skills and talents. Instead of seeking validation through external evaluations, focus on giving without expecting anything in return. This could mean volunteering or performing random acts of kindness. By offering your gifts without attachment to outcomes, you cultivate a greater sense of purpose and being. Your actions align with your true self, grounded in your spiritual being.

Initiate intentional grief work

Understand that the grieving process is not linear and it is normal to repeat and overlap feelings, emotions, and sensations. Seek feedback from trusted individuals who can provide additional perspectives that you may not be able to perceive on your own. Their insights can help shed light on areas that need further exploration and understanding.

Carve out dedicated time for self-reflection

Make self-reflection a priority by setting aside a specific time slot each day. Whether it's in the morning, during a midday break, or before bedtime, incorporating self-reflection into your daily routine reinforces its importance and ensures that you consistently engage in the practice.

By taking these physical actions for self-reflection, you empower yourself to navigate the challenges of loss, foster personal growth, and strengthen your emotional well-being. Remember, self-reflection is a journey, and by committing to these practices, you can find clarity, resilience, and understanding along the way.

Self-Reflection Homework Assignment

For one week, engage in a nightly routine of self-reflection. Dedicate 15 minutes to sit quietly and recall your day: the highlights, the challenges, and your responses to each situation. Journal your observations, focusing on your emotions, reactions, and areas for growth. At the end of the week, write a 100-word reflection summarizing your experience with this routine. Identify any patterns, insights, or emotional developments you've noticed. Reflect on how this exercise has influenced your understanding of yourself and your interactions with others.

Gratitude: Center on Joy Consistently

Gratitude is a powerful tool that encourages us to appreciate the blessings in our lives, fostering a positive mindset and nurturing our well-being. It goes beyond simply acknowledging the good, as it involves intentionally focusing on the positive moments, whether big or small, that occur in our daily lives.

By regularly practicing gratitude, we can improve our mood, foster resilience, reduce stress, and develop a broader perspective that allows us to see the positive aspects even during challenging times. It reminds us to center our attention on joy and embrace the abundance that surrounds us.

We will explore the numerous benefits of practicing gratitude and provide practical steps to incorporate it into our daily lives. By making gratitude a consistent part of our routine, we can cultivate a mindset of appreciation and experience the lasting rewards it brings to our overall well-being.

Emotional Targets: Appreciation, Peace, and Assurance

Embracing gratitude after experiencing loss provides a sense of grounding for you, allowing you to focus on the positive aspects of life even during challenging times. Adopting a grateful perspective helps you recognize the support and love that surrounds you, offering solace and healing. Intellect, judgment, and competence translate to appreciation, peace, assurance.

Appreciation: Apply rational thinking to analyze and understand the impact of gratitude on your well-being. Recognize that human nature inherently focuses on deficits and negative events. By actively shifting your focus toward appreciation and positivity, you can counterbalance this tendency and enhance your emotional health.

Peace: Make a conscious decision to practice gratitude, benefitting your emotional resilience and overall well-being. Weigh the potential advantages and assess your current mental state, avoiding excessive expectations or overthinking. Give gratitude a chance and allow it to positively influence your emotions following loss.

Assurance: Trust in the impact of gratitude on your emotional well-being, drawing from research, personal experience, and anecdotal evidence. Rely on credible sources and expert guidance to implement gratitude practices effectively and adapt them to your specific needs and circumstances. Add faith and achieve blessed assurance.

By embracing these emotional targets of appreciation, peace, and assurance, you actively cultivate gratitude as a mental habit and character element in your life. Through deliberate practice and a growth mindset, you experience the transformative power of gratitude, fostering emotional well-being and personal growth. With gratitude, you find solace, healing, and a renewed perspective amidst the challenges and losses you may face.

Physical Actions: Affirm You, Reframe, Post

To fully experience the benefits of gratitude, it is important to turn the emotional targets into tangible, actionable steps that you can incorporate into your daily routine. Here are practical strategies to cultivate gratitude in your life:

Affirmations: Set aside a few minutes each day to write down things you are grateful for. Start with simple and specific entries, such as a smile from a stranger or a favorite song. As time goes on, delve deeper into areas of gratitude, reflecting on meaningful relationships and milestones. Incorporate moments of gratitude into your daily routine, like expressing appreciation during meals or while commuting. By scheduling specific gratitude practices, you can make them an integral part of your life and gradually shift your mindset.

Reframe Challenging Situations: When faced with emotional distress or adversity, try to find the lessons or growth opportunities within them. Instead of fixating on the negatives, visualize how these experiences can contribute to your personal development or shape your future positively. Practice gratitude meditation for a few minutes each day, focusing on the things you are grateful for. Breathe deeply and reflect on each item, emotion, or person with gratitude and warmth. Regular meditation can help strengthen the neural pathways associated with gratitude and well-being.

Post Gratitude Reminders: Place visible reminders in your living space, such as quotes, pictures, or other inspirational items that remind you to appreciate the present and maintain a positive outlook, even during difficult times.

Extend your gratitude practice to your relationships with others. Develop a habit of acknowledging the kindness of others and expressing appreciation for their presence in your life. This can be done through heartfelt conversations, handwritten notes, or simple gestures of recognition.

By incorporating these practical gratitude strategies into your life, you can experience a powerful shift in perspective that contributes to emotional healing and personal growth. By embracing gratitude and taking physical actions towards it, you will be better equipped to navigate the complexities of loss and emerge stronger, wiser, and more resilient.

Gratitude Homework Assignment

For one week, practice the following gratitude exercise daily: Every night, list three specific things you are grateful for from the day. These can range from a pleasant interaction with someone to a beautiful sunset you witnessed. In addition to listing them, take a moment to reflect on each item and mentally express appreciation. After the one-week period, write a short reflection (around 100 words) on the impact this exercise had on your mood, emotional state, and overall well-being. Identify any noticeable changes and insights gained from this gratitude practice.

Flow: Finding the Balance for Growth and Enjoyment

Contentment vs. Complacency: Finding the Balance for Your Growth and Enjoyment

Sometimes, you may mistake contentment for complacency, believing that being satisfied with what you have means you don't want or need anything more. However, true contentment can coexist with your desire for growth and improvement. Let's explore this concept further.

Example 1: Your Kia Forte and the Cadillac Escalade Imagine you have a Kia Forte, and you find contentment in its ability to get you from point A to point B. However, if you were to upgrade to a Cadillac Escalade, your enjoyment would come from the additional benefits like being able to carry more people or things. This upgrade would align with your personal values and create gratitude without diminishing your contentment with the previous car.

Example 2: Your One-Bedroom Apartment and the Two-Bedroom   House Similarly, if you live in a one-bedroom apartment, you appreciate the shelter it provides and the way it enhances your life. But if you were to upgrade to a two-bedroom house, the joy would come from the added value that aligns with your personal values. This upgrade would open up new opportunities for gratitude and enjoyment.

This understanding is critical first and foremost because obtaining more possessions or achievements doesn't automatically guarantee happiness. It's important to realize that an upgrade is only considered as such when it aligns with your personal values and utility. It's not merely about acquiring more or reaching higher levels; it's about finding the significance and purpose that resonate with you. This awareness serves as the foundation for the universal invitation to strive for advancement, improvement, and self-satisfaction. By prioritizing utility and alignment with your values, you can embrace growth and fulfillment in a way that truly enhances your life.

Emotional Targets: Enjoyment & Maturity

Gratitude and Enjoyment: The Foundation of Your Contentment. Gratitude forms the foundation for your contentment and enjoyment. It goes beyond simply being satisfied with what you have and involves actively appreciating and relishing the present moment. This perspective allows for your growth, advancement, and self-satisfaction.

Example 3: Cultivating Gratitude. Cultivating gratitude involves recognizing the importance of the current moment and finding value in it. It's not about longing for something different or more, but rather about embracing your experience and making meaningful connections. By remaining open to the present moment, you cultivate a mindset of gratitude that lays the groundwork for your future enjoyment.

Lesson in Maturity: Balancing Your Contentment and Growth. Maturity teaches you that you can aspire without constantly striving for more. Make it an invitation rather than a task to do or goal to work toward. It's about finding a balance between your contentment and growth, embracing the opportunities for achievement while maintaining gratitude for your current circumstances. This lesson allows you to grow and evolve as an individual.

Lesson in Relationships: Embracing Alignment and Growth. In your relationships, you can continue to grow and develop with someone, even in the face of imperfections and setbacks. The key is to find someone who appreciates and celebrates the person you are, while also supporting your personal growth during challenging times. Building a relationship based on alignment of values and utility enables you to experience contentment while continuing to thrive.

Physical Actions: Integrating Alignment, Value, and Utility

Pattern of Flow: Moving Forward from Loss and Setbacks. When you face loss or setbacks, it doesn't mean the end of your potential for enjoyment and growth. Instead, it serves as a reset and an opportunity for you to realign with your personal values and utility. While it is natural to grieve the loss, establishing a new normal based on gratitude and alignment allows you to find continued enjoyment and fulfillment, propelling you forward in a state of flow.

Considerations of alignment, value, and utility deeply impact the experiences of gratitude, maturity, and flow. When you align your actions and choices with your core values and beliefs, gratitude becomes more profound. By recognizing the utility in the things and people in your life that align with your values, you cultivate a genuine appreciation and contentment.

Maturity, too, is enhanced by aligning with your values. As you mature, you understand that constant growth without purpose may not lead to lasting happiness. By embracing the values that matter to you, you make choices that truly contribute to your well-being and growth. This alignment allows you to gracefully navigate setbacks and losses, recognizing the lessons they bring and finding the resilience to move forward.

When you experience flow, the state of being fully absorbed and energized by a task, aligning with your values and considering utility is key. Engaging in activities that have meaning and purpose to you, where your skills align with the challenges at hand, brings about a sense of flow. In these moments, time seems to fade away as you effortlessly move towards your goals, experiencing deep fulfillment and accomplishment.

Considerations of alignment, value, and utility also play a crucial role in establishing a new normal after a loss or setback. While it's natural to grieve what you've lost, aligning with your values helps you find new meaning and purpose. You reassess your goals and actions, seeking utility in creating a new normal that reflects your revised perspective. By aligning with your values, you foster growth, contentment, and a renewed sense of fulfillment.

Homework Assignment: Reflecting on Transitions, Joy, and Momentum

Reflect on the concepts of transitions, joy, and momentum in relation to contentment and flow in your own life. Take a moment to consider moments when you have experienced transitions, found joy, and felt a sense of momentum that propelled you forward.

1. Reflect on transitions: Write a journal entry describing a significant transition you have experienced in your life. It could be a career change, a personal milestone, or any period of change. Reflect on how you navigated this transition, the emotions you felt, and how it impacted your

sense of contentment. Consider any lessons or insights you gained during this process.

2. Find joy in the present: Identify an activity or aspect of your life that brings you pure joy in the present moment. It could be something simple like cooking, painting, or spending time with loved ones. Write a paragraph explaining why this activity brings you joy and how it aligns with your values. Reflect on how this joy enhances your contentment and sense of flow.

3. Embrace momentum: Identify an area in your life where you feel a sense of momentum or forward progress. It could be a personal goal, a project, or a relationship. Write a brief paragraph outlining this area and how it is propelling you forward. Consider the enjoyment you derive from this momentum and how it contributes to your contentment and sense of flow.

Incorporate these reflections, joy, and momentum into your understanding of contentment and flow. By actively reflecting on transitions, finding joy in the present, and embracing momentum, you can cultivate a deeper understanding of how these elements contribute to your overall sense of contentment and enable you to experience a state of flow.

Section IV: Growth Habits

Growth Habits are the consistent practices and behaviors that individuals can incorporate into their daily lives to foster personal growth, build resilience, and adapt to change. The final section of the training focuses on the process of recovery, which involves personal growth, healing, and evolution. It provides guidance and support for participants as they navigate the challenges of loss and work towards building resilience, finding closure, and coping with grief.

Growth Habits
5. **Resourcefulness:** Use what you have to achieve what you want.
6. **Healing Space**: Continue to look for your tribe rather than attempting to fit.
7. **Productive Change:** Produce without aggression, without striving.
8. **Collaboration**: Create individual vision without isolating oneself from opportunities for collaboration.

Resourcefulness: How to Grow & Develop

The Question

How do you learn from something that is an incomplete lesson? The answer is in your vision and resources. Trust one. Develop the other.

Relationships are an integral part of our lives. We have relationships with family, friends, colleagues, and mentors. We have relationships with our spouses or partners, and we even have relationships with ourselves. Whether they are good or bad, they all have an impact on who we become.

The good news is that we can learn from all of them. The bad news is that sometimes those lessons are incomplete. In other words, there are some relationships where you don't get closure or get to say everything you want to say before the relationship ends. This can make it difficult for us to understand what went wrong or how we could have done things differently so that things had turned out differently for us.

But if you take a step back, it's easy to see that the fact that this relationship didn't turn out the way you wanted it to means one thing: You learned something from it! That doesn't mean everything was negative; in fact, most likely there were many positive aspects as well as some lessons learned along the way that will serve as a guidepost for future relationships down the road!

Trust Growth Like a Seed

"They buried us, but they didn't know we were seeds." Dinos Christianopoulos

If you've been through a breakup, or know someone who has, you know that the pain can be unbearable. But while it may seem like the end of the world at first, it's not necessarily the end of your world. In fact, there's a good chance that your relationship ending was for the best.

The obvious truth is that you weren't a good fit for each other in some way. Whether ghosted or not, fundamental differences exist between you and the other that made it impossible for you to stay together.

But even though things didn't work out with your ex, this doesn't mean that all hope is lost. In fact, it actually means that there's a lot of hope ahead. It means that you have an opportunity now to grow as an individual and to become happier with yourself than ever before!

The loss of this friendship was unexpected and painful. It was also an opportunity to learn things about myself and how I want to impact others. Personal growth comes from an understanding of your unique contribution to the world. After identifying your contribution, you find your vehicle--one that fits who you are and how you work. Then, be consistent and watch your impact.

Developing Resources

"When someone shows you who they are, believe them." Maya Angelou

When you lose someone close to you, it feels like your world has been turned upside down. In some cases, it can take years to get back on track again and many people never get there at all. However, if you can accept this relationship loss as a gift instead of a curse, it will change your life forever for the better!

Work to envision a reality and cultivate cognitive and character resources that will always be your foundation no matter what happens in your life. Losing someone doesn't require that you wish them ill. Respect them and their choices to walk their own path right. To you, I say do not worry about the loss of closure. I have seen too many come back around whether in apology, attempted reconnection, or otherwise trading on their own terms. More important than this wonder and worry, instead of waiting around for them, prioritize You. The physical pain will subside even as the emotional hurt lingers. But each heartbeat reminds you of the resources that you have on hand for your best life and the journey ahead.

Look back at the lessons presented within this volume. Grow your reasoning capacity beyond simple needs and answers from others. Begin to create the narrative, the processes, and indeed the science of your healing. Present it as a roadmap for others. Develop your character traits as an expression of You. Develop a solid identity with an I AM statement that stands up to the detractors, narcissists, and second-guessing. Be who you are without apology even while open to growth and development in all areas.

The journey of healing is a complex and multifaceted process that involves the interplay of narrative, processes, and science. By understanding each of these components and their roles in healing, individuals can better navigate their own path to recovery, growth, and well-being.

Narrative: The stories we tell ourselves about our past experiences and future aspirations play a crucial role in the healing process. Our narratives help us make sense of our experiences, integrate them into our sense of self, and shape our beliefs about what is possible for us moving forward. To heal, it is important to examine and reframe our narratives, acknowledging the challenges we have faced while also recognizing our strengths, resilience, and capacity for growth. By cultivating a more empowering narrative, we can foster a sense of hope and trust in our ability to create a better future.

Processes: The healing process involves various practices and activities that support self-development and emotional processing. These processes can include:

- **Time**: Allowing ourselves the time and space to process our emotions, reflect on our experiences, and gain perspective on our situation.
- **Space**: Creating a safe and supportive environment, both physically and emotionally, where we can explore our feelings, thoughts, and beliefs without judgment.
- **Recreation**: Engaging in activities that bring joy, relaxation, and a sense of accomplishment, which can help counterbalance the pain and challenges we face during the healing process.
- **Feeling the pain**: Acknowledging and allowing ourselves to experience the full range of emotions, including pain, sadness, anger, and grief, as an essential part of the healing journey.

Science: The science of healing encompasses various fields of study, including grief, growth, gratitude, and evolution. These areas of research provide valuable insights into the mechanisms and factors that contribute to healing and personal development.

- **Grief**: The study of grief helps us understand the stages, emotions, and coping strategies associated with loss and bereavement. This knowledge can inform therapeutic interventions and support systems that facilitate the grieving process.
- **Growth**: Research on personal growth and development sheds light on the factors that contribute to resilience, adaptability, and the ability to learn from adversity. This information can help individuals cultivate the skills and mindsets necessary for healing and growth.
- **Gratitude**: The science of gratitude explores the benefits of cultivating a grateful mindset, such as increased well-being, improved relationships, and enhanced coping skills. By practicing gratitude, individuals can foster a more positive outlook and enhance their overall healing process.
- **Evolution**: The study of human evolution and the adaptive mechanisms that have shaped our species can provide insights into the innate capacities for healing and growth that we possess. This understanding can help us tap into our inherent strengths and resilience as we navigate the healing journey.

In conclusion, the journey of healing is a dynamic and multifaceted process that involves the integration of narrative, processes, and science. By understanding and engaging with each of these components, individuals can better navigate their own path to recovery, growth, and well-being.

Homework: Resourcefulness

Assignment: Identify a challenge or goal you are currently facing. Make a list of resources that you already have at your disposal, such as skills, knowledge, connections, and assets. Brainstorm creative ways to use these resources to overcome the challenge or achieve the goal. Reflect on how being resourceful can help you in various aspects of your life.

Emotional Space: Facing Your Greatest Fear

The Question

It is not unusual to be afraid of being alone, but it is important to realize that being alone is a choice. The question you must ask yourself is this: Can you release the fear of losing them and trust that losing them is better than losing yourself?

The answer requires you to get comfortable being alone knowing that, if you should find yourself alone, you are in good company. The self-love required is expression of your purpose without limits.

You are meant to live a life beyond comparison or competition. You are not here to compete with anyone else or compare yourself to anyone else. You are here to love and support others as they go through their own journey of life. You cannot do that if you are so focused on what other people think about you or how they might judge you for your choices.

Loving Alone

"It is easy in the world to live after the world's opinion; it is easy in solitude to live after our own; but the great man is he who in the midst of the crowd keeps with perfect sweetness the independence of solitude." Ralph Waldo Emerson

Being Good Company. When you are in a relationship, you make compromises. You give up parts of yourself to be with the other person. You put your needs and wants on hold so that they can have what they want. This is how love works in the beginning, but if you don't do anything about it, it will slowly turn into resentment.

The problem with resenting someone for something they didn't do is that you're stuck with them forever. You can't get rid of them and move on with your life because you're too afraid of being alone. The truth is that being alone isn't so bad once you get used to it! You don't need anyone else to feel happy or fulfilled; it's all within yourself.

Once you realize this, breaking up becomes easier. You don't have to worry about hurting their feelings or making them sad because they weren't good enough for you — they weren't good enough because they weren't making you happy! And they weren't making you happy because they were draining your energy every day by asking for things from you that were not right for either one of your lives.

Not Just Activities but Purpose. The fear of being alone can be more powerful than any other fear in the world. That's why so many people stay in relationships where they don't feel good about themselves. They'd rather be miserable with someone else than alone by themselves. But another phrasing of the alone question is to ask, "How important is living a life of purpose?" If the compromises you have made were loss of You and denial, barrier, or hurdles to your purpose, it is too much of a price to bear.

Making Your Mark. You are wonderful and becoming better each day that you rise with consistent effort toward learning, growth, and development. You are enough. You are deserving of the best. You have purpose. You can contribute to the world. Your mark is your impact that lasts beyond your time spent and exponentially expands through the lives you touch. Do not lose sight of this opportunity. If you have lost it, let's work each day to reclaim it through acceptance, affirmation, exploration, and practice—all activities that are perfect to engage alone or with trusted and professional help.

Relationships are inherently messy. They challenge us, they pull us out of our comfort zone, and they make us vulnerable. This reminds us that relationships are also an opportunity for growth. Relationships can be so challenging because they require us to stay present in the moment and fail to plan, or we are so focused on the promise of what lies ahead that we fail to address the present concerns. Neither focus is right or wrong. Only the failures are problematic. You may have a great relationship but still find yourself struggling. You may be working on a project but find yourself stuck in a rut because your effort is misplaced.

After a breakup, your brain is working overtime to make sense of what happened. Your focus is on understanding. For this you need information. You seek this information from the other. The focus on what is happening now is not the problem. The problem is that you may fail to see how much more there is to gain by looking ahead. You lost when you got so caught up in the details of the relationship that you forget about your self-development and your dreams. Relationships that cost our full potential are missing the mark even when they feel good.

Homework: Healing Space

Assignment: Reflect on the characteristics of your ideal "tribe" or supportive community. Consider the values, interests, and goals that you would like to share with this group. Then, research and identify at least three local or online groups, clubs, or organizations that align with your ideal community. Make plans to attend a meeting or event for at least one of these groups to start building connections with like-minded individuals.

Productive Change: Purpose as Expression of Self-Love

"Love of self and love of life connects us with the prosperity of the Universe. Self-love creates self-expression and allows us to be creative in deeply fulfilling ways." Louise Hay

Defining Purpose for You Without Them

I remember the story of a person who, in a relationship, shared their budding thoughts with their significant other. The other was a cautiously supportive person whose approach was heavy on planning, preparation, and double checking. The other also had their own projects. Caution came through loud and clear while support was much less pronounced.

At least two lessons are evident here. The first lesson is about protecting your ideas until they are in prototype form. Sharing ideas when they are budding and fragile can cut them off before they bear fruit. The second lesson is to build your own support and inspiration without others. Your inspiration must carry the day. A life without limits must be perpetually powered by your inspiration.

Removing Limits

You don't see it as a limitation but considering them first is a limitation that you cannot afford. The resultant push forward despite them with purpose as primary serves them more than any other option. In this purpose primary approach, they are not a hindrance, excuse, or obstacle. They are never to be resented. And if they do not understand and insist on standing in your way, you know that they are not the Ying to your soul's Yang. Their position must be reset and relegated to another seat in your life. Your purpose is indeed more important than them or anyone. It is an expression of you that must not be stifled.

Limitless: Blaming You & Producing

The harsh realization comes when you don't have anyone to blame but yourself. When you are sitting in the midst of solitude lacking the motivation to put pen to paper, glue gun to craft, or needle to fabric. When you face the fact that you are the problem and the solution, that is when you have the greatest choice. You know it can be devastating if you flinch but allow me to focus on the process of standing confident, defiant even in the face of this choice.

1. Define for certain what you want to achieve and the habits that support that reality.
2. Align your energy as well as measure the amount you will spend.
3. Identify the solution you provide to the problem you perceive.
4. Ensure that your work on the solution fits with what you love to do and find enjoyment doing.
5. Systematically, in the context of a business model, grow your impact. The money will come.

Embarking on a journey of productive change requires clarity, alignment, and a systematic approach to growth. The following steps will guide you through the process of achieving productive change and realizing your goals:

Step 1: Define Your Habits
You would think that you should plan with goals. A more fruitful way to think of your goals is to consider the habits that demonstrate them. Start by choosing to define, with certainty, what you want to achieve. This involves setting clear and specific goals that reflect your passions and values. Take the time to reflect on your aspirations and write them down. Ensure they are realistic and achievable by considering the habits you must incorporate into your day toward achieving them. Consider, "If my goal was being met each day, what behaviors would people see from me?"

Step 2: Align Your Energy and Resources
Align your energy and resources with your goals by determining the amount of effort, time, and money you are willing to invest in achieving them. This step involves creating a plan that outlines the necessary resources and ensures you are committed to investing in your success. For your people resource, create a schedule of connections and networking. For your financial resources, create a budget—know what you will spend and where your will not spend. For your information resources, create a schedule of learning and brainstorming. Include a journal or digital way to record your thoughts and ideas. For your time resource, balance recreation, reflection, work, and physical health activities.

Step 3: Identify the Solution You Provide
Articulate the problem you are aiming to solve and identify the solution you can provide. This step involves recognizing the value you bring to the table and how your unique skills, talents, and ideas can

contribute to addressing the issue at hand. The crucial element to financial sustainability is to provide something people will pay for. It is not the fad or trend watching you may think it is. Your task is to discover what you uniquely can address in the market.

Step 4: Ensure Your Work Aligns with Your Passions

Make sure that the work you do on your chosen solution aligns with your passions and interests—those tasks and machinations you enjoy rising in the morning and doing. This is crucial for maintaining motivation and enjoying the process of productive change. When you love what you do and find enjoyment in it, you are more likely to stay committed and achieve your goals.

Step 5: Implement a Business Model for Growth

Systematically grow your impact by developing and implementing a business model that supports your goals. This step involves identifying the key components of your business, such as revenue streams, target audience, and marketing strategies. Simply put, know the mechanism of making your money. As you grow your impact, focus on providing value and solving problems, and the financial rewards will follow.

Beyond Loss: The You

You may have noticed that the discussion has turned away from your hurt and loss. This is not about finding them. This is about finding You. Achieving productive change involves defining your goals, aligning your energy and resources, identifying the solution you provide, ensuring your work aligns with your passions, and implementing a business model for growth. By following these steps, you can embark on a journey of personal and professional growth that leads to lasting success and fulfillment. You are preparing for life and that more abundantly. Whether you engage in a romantic relationship, business relationship; long-term or short-term; intense or casual, you will be more sustainably happy and competently discerning because of the productive change that is self-awareness and evolution in You.

From this moment forward, make the way for this activity of purpose to fully consume your life. That means ordering all activities in service to this ideal. Exercise, diet, relationships, recreation, and everything else must serve your purpose. There is more than happiness there. Therein is legacy. Therein is immortality.

Your I AM Statement

Developing a solid "I AM" statement is essential for maintaining a strong sense of self, even when faced with external pressures to conform or suppress your emotions. By embracing your authentic identity and remaining open to growth and development, you can navigate life's challenges with resilience and confidence. Here's a guide to creating a comprehensive "I AM" statement:

Identity Statement: Define who you are at your core, considering your values, passions, and unique qualities. This statement should reflect your authentic self, independent of external influences or expectations.

Example: I am a compassionate, creative, and determined individual who values honesty, empathy, and personal growth.

Purpose Statement: Describe your overarching purpose or mission in life, considering your passions, strengths, and the impact you want to have on the world.

Example: My purpose is to inspire and empower others to embrace their authenticity and cultivate a deep sense of self-worth through my work as a coach, writer, and speaker.

Intention & Vision: Outline your intentions and vision for your personal and professional life, focusing on what you want to achieve, experience, and contribute.

Example: I intend to create a thriving coaching practice that supports individuals in their personal growth journeys, while also writing a book and giving talks to share my message on a larger scale.

Competence Presentation: Showcase your skills, knowledge, and expertise, demonstrating your ability to effectively pursue your goals and make a positive impact.

Example: I have a degree in psychology, years of experience working in personal development, and a strong track record of helping clients overcome challenges and achieve their goals.

Flow Statement (Allowing and Attracting): Emphasize your openness to growth, learning, and attracting new opportunities, while also acknowledging your inherent worthiness and the importance of self-compassion.

Example: I am committed to continuous learning and growth, embracing new experiences and opportunities with an open heart and mind. I trust in my ability to navigate challenges and believe in my inherent worthiness to achieve my dreams.

By crafting a comprehensive "I AM" statement that encompasses your identity, purpose, vision, competence, and openness to growth, you can maintain a strong sense of self even when faced with pressure to conform or deny your feelings. Embrace your unique identity without apology, while also remaining open to growth and development in all areas of your life.

Homework: Productive Change

Assignment: Choose a personal or professional goal that you are currently working towards. For one week, practice a non-striving approach to this goal by focusing on the process rather than the outcome. Keep a daily journal to document your experiences, noting any changes in your stress levels, satisfaction, and overall well-being. At the end of the week, reflect on the impact of this approach and consider how you can apply it to other areas of your life.

Collaboration: Enjoying More, Striving Less

"It's when we start working together that the real healing takes place."
— David Hume

"Healing requires from us to stop struggling, but to enjoy life more and endure it less."
— Darina Stoyanova

Collaboration is a powerful tool for personal growth, healing, and evolution. By working together, we can create meaningful connections, foster innovation, and achieve our shared goals. By embracing a collaborative mindset and following the steps outlined above, we can enjoy more, strive less, and ultimately, create a brighter future for ourselves and those around us.

Foundation for Working Together

So, back to relationships. Health must be about building. Not about getting together only to produce babies, but to produce something tangible for influence in the world that would not be possible through either of you separately. The crucial point is that this can be platonic relationships as well as romantic relationships. This must be your focus in employment relationships as well as banking contracts. Ask, "What can we build together?" and expect a solid response.

To fully embrace collaboration, it's important to cultivate a mindset that values teamwork, open communication, and mutual respect. This involves:

Being open to new ideas and perspectives: Embracing collaboration requires a willingness to consider different viewpoints and approaches. This openness allows for the integration of diverse ideas, leading to more innovative and effective solutions. By being receptive to new thoughts and opinions, collaborators can learn from one another and develop a richer understanding of the issues at hand.

Actively listening to the thoughts and concerns of others: Active listening involves giving full attention to the speaker, seeking to understand their message, and responding thoughtfully. This skill is essential for effective collaboration, as it fosters empathy, builds trust, and ensures that everyone's voice is heard. By genuinely engaging with the ideas and concerns of others, collaborators can work together more cohesively and address potential challenges more effectively.

Recognizing and appreciating the contributions of each team member: Successful collaboration relies on the unique skills, knowledge, and experiences of everyone. By acknowledging and valuing the input of every team member, collaborators create a positive and motivating atmosphere where everyone feels valued and respected. This appreciation fosters a sense of ownership and commitment to the shared goals, ultimately enhancing the overall performance of the team.

Encouraging a supportive and inclusive environment: A collaborative mindset emphasizes the importance of creating a safe and supportive space where all team members feel comfortable sharing their thoughts and ideas. This involves promoting open communication, providing constructive feedback, and offering encouragement and assistance when needed. By fostering an inclusive environment, collaborators can work together more effectively and overcome challenges with a sense of unity and shared purpose.

Embracing diversity and valuing the unique strengths of everyone: A diverse team brings together a wide range of skills, experiences, and perspectives that can greatly enhance the collaborative process. By embracing and celebrating these differences, collaborators can leverage the unique strengths of everyone to generate innovative solutions and achieve better results. Furthermore, valuing diversity promotes a culture of inclusion and respect, which is essential for maintaining a healthy and productive collaborative environment.

Non-Striving is Healthy

Healing in this context is not about redressing the past. It is about securing a future through intentional investment in the present. This approach allows you to take each moment in stride, placing one step confidently in front of the other as you commit to moving forward. No worry about the competition, the external chaos, or trends without a grounding in your joy, interests, and passion.

When individuals come together with a shared vision and complementary skills, they can achieve far more than they could alone.

Collaboration fosters creativity, innovation, and growth, allowing each person to contribute their unique talents and perspectives to the project.

By working together, collaborators can overcome obstacles, learn from one another, and create something truly exceptional. This collaborative approach aligns with the concept of non-striving, which emphasizes the importance of allowing things to unfold naturally without forcing or struggling to achieve specific outcomes. When we embrace the law of attraction, we focus on cultivating positive thoughts, emotions, and beliefs that attract the experiences we desire.

This perspective encourages us to trust the process, remain open to opportunities, and let go of the need to control every aspect of our lives. By combining the power of collaboration with a non-striving attitude and the principles of the law of attraction, we can create an environment where success, growth, and personal fulfillment emerge organically, without the stress and pressure typically associated with traditional goal setting and achievement.

Steps to Negotiating a Healthy Collaboration

1. **Ask, "What can we Build together?"**: Start by initiating a conversation with potential collaborators about what you can create together. This question opens up the possibilities for a shared vision and sets the stage for a productive partnership.

2. **Answer with your contribution to the team and where you need help**: Be honest and clear about your strengths and areas of expertise, as well as where you need support from others. This transparency allows for a balanced and effective collaboration.

3. **Review the plan to assess whether the team has the expertise needed**: Once you have a clear understanding of each person's contributions, evaluate whether the team has the

necessary skills and knowledge to achieve the shared goals. If there are gaps, consider how they can be addressed.

4. **Engage additional help if needed**: If your assessment reveals that the team lacks specific expertise, seek out additional collaborators who can fill those gaps. This may involve reaching out to your network, hiring consultants, or partnering with other organizations.

5. **Schedule evaluation points as conversations for challenging and cheerleading periodically throughout the production process**: Regularly check in with your team to assess progress, discuss challenges, and celebrate successes. These evaluation points serve as opportunities to refine the collaboration, address any issues, and maintain momentum.

Homework: Collaboration

Assignment: Identify a project or goal that you believe could benefit from collaboration with others. Write a brief description of your vision for this project, as well as the skills, knowledge, and resources that you can contribute. Next, make a list of potential collaborators, including friends, colleagues, or members of your network who have complementary skills or interests. Reach out to at least one of these individuals to discuss the possibility of working together on the project and explore how collaboration can help you achieve your goals while maintaining your individual vision.